MASTERING YOUR

FINANCES

A Comprehensive Guide To Effective

Money Management

By

Brain Sethi

TABLE OF CONTENTS:

CHAPTER 1

Introduction

CHAPTER 1

INTRODUCTION:

Welcome to "Mastering Your Finances: A Comprehensive Guide to Effective Money Management." In an era where financial landscapes are constantly evolving, the need for sound financial mastery has never been more crucial. This book is designed to be your trusted companion on the journey toward achieving a state of financial well-being, offering practical insights and strategies to empower you in taking control of your financial destiny.

In this comprehensive guide, we will delve into the foundations of financial success, providing you with the tools to cultivate a resilient financial mindset and set clear, achievable goals. From the essential aspects of budgeting and income optimization to the complexities of investing and retirement planning, each chapter is crafted to equip you with the knowledge and skills necessary to navigate the intricate world of personal finance.

We will explore actionable steps for managing debt, implementing effective saving strategies, and understanding the nuances of insurance and tax planning. Along the way, you'll discover the importance of financial milestones and learn how to maintain financial health through regular checkups and adjustments.

As we journey together through the pages of this guide, our aim is not just to impart knowledge but to inspire confidence. Whether you're starting on the path to financial mastery or looking to enhance your existing financial skills, this book is your roadmap to achieving sustainable financial success. Let's embark on this transformative journey, where you will gain the insights needed to make informed decisions, overcome financial challenges, and ultimately, master your finances.

In the ever-changing landscape of personal finance, the ability to master your finances is a skill that transcends economic climates. This book recognizes the diverse challenges individuals face and serves as a comprehensive guide to empower you at every stage of your financial journey.

Financial mastery is not about amassing wealth for its own sake; it's about achieving a state of balance, security, and fulfillment. It's understanding the intricate dance between earning, saving, investing, and planning for the future. Whether you're striving for financial independence, planning for major life events, or simply seeking to gain control over your financial narrative, the principles outlined in this guide are tailored to meet your unique needs.

We'll explore the art of budgeting, demystify the world of investments, and equip you with the tools to make informed decisions about your money. As we navigate through the chapters, you'll discover that mastering your finances is not a one-size-fits-all endeavor. Instead, it's a personalized journey, and this guide aims to provide you with the knowledge and strategies to craft a financial plan that aligns with your aspirations.

Moreover, we'll discuss the importance of resilience in the face of unexpected challenges and provide guidance on building a financial legacy that extends beyond your lifetime. Through real-world examples, practical tips, and interactive exercises, you'll be encouraged to not only understand the principles but also apply them in your day-to-day life.

So, whether you're just beginning your financial journey or looking to refine your existing strategies, join us in this exploration of financial mastery. Let's embark together on a transformative odyssey towards lasting financial success and well-being.

Introduction to Foundations of Financial Success:

In the vast landscape of personal finance, the journey towards mastery begins with a strong foundation. This chapter, "Foundations of Financial Success," serves as the bedrock for your exploration into the principles and practices that underpin a resilient and prosperous financial future.

Financial success is not merely a destination; it's a dynamic process shaped by your mindset, knowledge, and intentional actions. This chapter is designed to guide you through the fundamental aspects that contribute to building a sturdy financial foundation—one that withstands the tests of time and economic fluctuations.

We commence with the exploration of the pivotal role played by your financial mindset. Understanding how your beliefs and attitudes influence your financial decisions is key to unlocking a path towards resilience and adaptability in the face of challenges. We'll delve into the concept of financial resilience, illuminating ways to navigate setbacks and transform them into opportunities for growth.

Moreover, we emphasize the ongoing importance of financial education in your journey. In a world where financial landscapes evolve rapidly, equipping yourself with knowledge becomes a cornerstone of informed decision-making. We'll discuss strategies to stay abreast of financial trends, investment strategies, and best practices, empowering you to make sound financial choices.

As we progress, we'll explore the symbiotic relationship between personal growth and financial success. Embracing a mindset of continuous improvement opens doors to innovative solutions and increased earning potential. We'll unravel the powerful connection between personal development and financial well-being.

Lastly, we'll delve into the transformative power of visualization and affirmations. These tools, often overlooked, hold the potential to shape your financial reality. By creating vivid mental images of your financial goals and reinforcing positive beliefs through affirmations, you lay the groundwork for aligning your actions with your aspirations.

Join us on this exploration of the Foundations of Financial Success—a journey that goes beyond balance sheets and numbers. It's a journey into the heart of your financial mindset, knowledge, and growth, setting the stage for a resilient and prosperous financial future.

CHAPTER 2
FOUNDATIONS OF FINANCIAL SUCCESS

In the intricate world of personal finance, success is built upon a solid foundation. This chapter lays the groundwork for your journey toward financial mastery by exploring the fundamental principles that form the bedrock of financial success.

Building a Strong Financial Mindset: Understanding the psychology behind financial decisions is paramount. We delve into the importance of cultivating a positive and resilient financial mindset. Learn how to overcome common money-related anxieties, embrace a growth-oriented approach, and foster a mindset that sets the stage for financial well-being.

Setting Clear Financial Goals: Goals act as the compass on your financial journey. In this section, we explore the art of setting clear, achievable financial goals. Whether you're aiming for short-term milestones or envisioning your long-term financial future, we provide practical techniques for defining, refining, and prioritizing your objectives.

As we navigate through these foundational aspects, you'll gain insights into how mindset shapes financial behaviors and discover the transformative power of intentional goal-setting. By laying a robust foundation, you're not just preparing for financial success; you're creating a framework that will guide your decisions, shape your habits, and empower you on your path to mastering your finances.

Cultivating a Resilient Financial Mindset: Your mindset is the lens through which you view and interact with your financial reality. This section explores the concept of financial resilience—a mindset that enables you to adapt to challenges, bounce back from setbacks, and stay focused on your long-term objectives. Uncover strategies for reframing financial setbacks as learning opportunities and embracing a positive, solution-oriented approach to money matters.

Understanding the Role of Financial Education: Knowledge is a key pillar of financial success. We delve into the importance of ongoing financial education and provide resources for staying informed about economic trends, investment strategies, and personal finance best practices. Equip yourself with the tools to make informed decisions, navigate financial complexities, and stay ahead in an ever-evolving financial landscape.

Embracing a Growth-Oriented Approach: In the realm of personal finance, growth is not just about accumulating wealth; it's about continuous improvement and learning. This section explores the connection between personal development and financial success. Discover how adopting a growth-oriented mindset can lead to innovative solutions, increased earning potential, and a more fulfilling financial journey.

The Power of Visualization and Affirmations: Visualization and affirmations are powerful tools for manifesting financial success. Learn how to create a clear mental image of your financial goals and use positive affirmations to reinforce your beliefs in your ability to achieve them. By incorporating these techniques into your daily routine, you can align your actions with your aspirations and cultivate a mindset geared for success.

As we delve deeper into the foundations of financial success, remember that mastering your finances is not only about the numbers; it's about cultivating a mindset that empowers you to make wise decisions, persevere through challenges, and build a resilient foundation for lasting financial well-being.

CHAPTER 3
BUDGETING BASICS

Effective budgeting is the cornerstone of financial success, providing a roadmap for managing income, expenses, and achieving your financial goals. In this chapter, we will delve into the fundamental principles of budgeting, empowering you to take control of your finances with confidence.

Creating a Personal Budget: Discover the art of crafting a personalized budget tailored to your unique financial situation. We will guide you through the process of identifying sources of income, categorizing expenses, and setting realistic spending limits. Learn practical tips for creating a budget that aligns with your financial goals, allowing you to allocate resources efficiently and cultivate a sense of financial discipline.

Tracking and Managing Expenses: Understanding where your money goes is essential for informed decision-making. Explore effective strategies for tracking and categorizing expenses, gaining insights into your spending patterns. We'll introduce tools and techniques to simplify expense management, ensuring that you stay in control of your financial narrative and can make adjustments as needed.

As we navigate through the intricacies of budgeting, you'll gain not only the practical skills to create and manage a budget but also a deeper understanding of how this fundamental practice forms the basis for achieving financial stability and success. The principles outlined in this chapter will serve as a solid framework, empowering you to make intentional financial choices and navigate the complexities of your financial journey with clarity and purpose.

Understanding Your Financial Flow: Before creating a budget, it's crucial to comprehend your financial inflows and outflows. We'll explore methods for accurately assessing your income sources, including fixed and variable earnings. Understanding the ebb and flow of your finances is essential for creating a realistic budget that accommodates both regular expenses and variable costs.

Emergency Fund: Your Budget's Safety Net: Within the realm of budgeting, we emphasize the significance of establishing and maintaining an emergency fund. This financial safety net acts as a buffer against unexpected expenses, providing peace of mind and stability. Learn how to integrate an emergency fund seamlessly into your budget, ensuring you're prepared for life's uncertainties without compromising your financial goals.

Budgeting for Short-Term and Long-Term Goals:
Budgeting isn't just about managing day-to-day expenses; it's a dynamic tool for achieving your financial aspirations. Explore the concept of allocating funds for short-term goals such as vacations or home improvements, as well as long-term goals like buying a home, education, or retirement. We'll guide you in creating a budget that aligns with your unique financial objectives, allowing you to balance current needs with future aspirations.

Adapting Your Budget to Life Changes: Life is dynamic, and so should be your budget. Discover strategies for adapting your budget to accommodate major life changes such as career transitions, marriage, or parenthood. We'll provide practical insights on how to modify your budget to reflect changing priorities, ensuring that your financial plan remains flexible and resilient in the face of evolving circumstances.

By the end of this chapter, you will not only have the practical tools to create and manage a budget effectively but also the strategic understanding of how budgeting acts as a dynamic and adaptable tool on your journey toward financial mastery. Embrace the power of budgeting as a means to achieve your short-term objectives, safeguard against uncertainties, and build a

strong foundation for long-term financial success.

CHAPTER 4
INCOME OPTIMIZATION

Optimizing your income is a pivotal step in the pursuit of financial mastery. In this chapter, we explore strategies and principles that empower you to maximize your earning potential, creating a solid foundation for effective money management.

Strategies for Increasing Your Income: Unlock the potential for financial growth by delving into practical strategies to increase your income. Whether you're exploring opportunities for career advancement, negotiating salary increases, or considering additional income streams, this section provides actionable insights to boost your earning capacity.

Maximizing Earning Potential: Understanding the nuances of your profession or industry is key to maximizing your earning potential. We'll discuss the importance of continuous skill development, networking, and positioning yourself strategically in the job market. Discover how staying informed about industry trends and cultivating a proactive approach can lead to opportunities for advancement and increased income.

As we explore the realm of income optimization, you'll gain not only a deeper understanding of the strategies for increasing your income but also a mindset geared toward proactive career management. This chapter is designed to empower you to take control of your financial destiny by leveraging your skills, knowledge, and opportunities to achieve sustainable financial success.

Diversifying Income Streams: Creating financial resilience involves diversifying your income sources. We'll explore the concept of multiple income streams and provide insights into various avenues such as side hustles, investments, or passive income. By diversifying your income, you not only enhance your financial stability but also open doors to new opportunities and potential growth.

Entrepreneurial Ventures: For those with an entrepreneurial spirit, this section explores the intricacies of starting and managing your own business. From ideation to execution, we'll cover key considerations for entrepreneurs, including market research, business planning, and financial management. Whether you're launching a startup or exploring freelancing opportunities, this chapter equips you with the knowledge to navigate the entrepreneurial landscape.

Negotiation and Career Advancement: Maximizing your income often involves effective negotiation and strategic career advancement. We'll delve into the art of negotiation, offering practical tips on salary discussions, contract terms, and performance reviews. Additionally, explore strategies for career advancement, including skill development, networking, and positioning yourself for promotions.

Continuous Learning and Skill Development: In today's dynamic job market, staying relevant is paramount. This section emphasizes the importance of continuous learning and skill development. Discover resources and strategies for upgrading your skills, whether through formal education, online courses, or on-the-job training. By investing in your professional growth, you enhance your value in the workplace, potentially leading to increased earning opportunities.

Balancing Passion and Profit: Optimizing your income isn't solely about financial gain; it's also about aligning your work with your passions. Explore ways to identify and pursue opportunities that not only provide financial rewards but also align with your personal and professional interests. Balancing passion and profit creates a fulfilling career trajectory while maximizing your income potential.

As we journey through the intricacies of income optimization, remember that financial success is not solely about earning more; it's about making intentional choices that align with your values and goals. This chapter equips you with the tools to navigate the diverse landscape of income optimization, empowering you to craft a career that not only sustains your financial well-being but also fulfills your aspirations.

CHAPTER 5
DEBT MANAGEMENT

Effectively managing debt is a critical aspect of mastering your finances. In this chapter, we explore strategies and principles to help you navigate and conquer debt, paving the way for a more secure financial future.

Tackling Debt Head-On: Understanding the types of debt and their implications is the first step toward effective debt management. We'll delve into distinguishing between good and bad debt, examining interest rates, and providing a framework for prioritizing repayment. Learn how to create a clear picture of your debt landscape and develop a strategic plan for tackling outstanding balances.

Developing a Debt Repayment Plan: This section guides you through the process of creating a personalized debt repayment plan. Whether you're dealing with credit card debt, student loans, or other liabilities, we'll explore popular methods such as the debt snowball and debt avalanche. You'll gain insights into negotiating with creditors, refinancing options, and creating a sustainable repayment schedule that aligns with your financial goals.

Building Healthy Credit Habits: Your credit history plays a significant role in your financial health. Explore the importance of maintaining a positive credit score and cultivating healthy credit habits. We'll provide tips for monitoring your credit report, understanding credit utilization, and making strategic financial decisions that contribute to a positive credit profile.

Emergency Debt Strategies: Unexpected financial challenges can sometimes lead to increased debt. This section addresses strategies for managing debt during emergencies, such as medical expenses or job loss. Discover how to build an emergency fund as a buffer and navigate challenging situations without compromising your long-term financial goals.

Debt-Free Mindset: Achieving a debt-free mindset involves not only practical strategies but also a shift in perspective. Explore the psychological aspects of debt and learn how to cultivate a mindset focused on financial freedom. By adopting a debt-free mentality, you'll gain the resilience and determination needed to overcome challenges and build a sustainable, debt-free future.

As we delve into the complexities of debt management, remember that conquering debt is a powerful step toward financial mastery. This chapter equips you with the tools and knowledge to not only eliminate existing debt but also foster habits that prevent future financial challenges, allowing you to move confidently toward a more financially secure future.

Understanding Interest Rates and Fees: To effectively manage debt, it's crucial to comprehend the impact of interest rates and associated fees. This section provides a comprehensive overview of how interest accrues, the difference between fixed and variable rates, and how fees can contribute to overall debt. Armed with this knowledge, you'll be better equipped to make informed decisions about prioritizing and paying down your debts.

Consolidation Strategies: For individuals managing multiple debts, consolidation can be a valuable strategy. We'll explore debt consolidation options, including balance transfers, personal loans, and debt consolidation programs. This section guides you through the pros and cons of each method, empowering you to choose the strategy that aligns with your financial goals and circumstances.

Negotiating with Creditors: Facing financial hardship doesn't mean you're without options. This part of the chapter dives into the art of negotiating with creditors. Learn effective communication strategies, understand hardship programs, and discover how negotiating can lead to more manageable repayment terms. Negotiation can be a powerful tool for regaining control over your financial situation.

Refinancing and Loan Restructuring: In certain situations, refinancing or restructuring loans may provide relief. We'll explore the considerations and steps involved in refinancing, including potential benefits and drawbacks. Understanding when and how to restructure loans can be a proactive approach to managing debt while optimizing your financial resources.

Credit Counseling and Professional Assistance: Sometimes, seeking professional guidance is the most prudent choice. This section introduces credit counseling services and outlines the benefits of working with financial professionals. Explore how credit counselors can provide personalized advice, negotiate with creditors on your behalf, and guide you toward a debt-free future.

Remember, the goal of debt management is not just about repaying what you owe but also about building a foundation for lasting financial well-being. This chapter provides comprehensive insights into the intricacies of debt management, offering practical tools and strategies to empower you on the path to financial freedom.

CHAPTER 6
SAVING STRATEGIES

Building a robust savings strategy is a key pillar of effective money management. In this chapter, we'll explore a variety of saving strategies designed to help you grow your wealth, establish financial security, and achieve your long-term financial goals.

The Power of Saving: Emergency Fund and Beyond:
We begin by emphasizing the importance of an emergency fund—a financial safety net that provides stability during unexpected events. Learn how to determine the ideal size of your emergency fund, where to store it, and why having this financial cushion is crucial for maintaining control over your finances, especially during unforeseen circumstances.

Smart Saving Habits for Long-Term Goals: Saving isn't just about preparing for emergencies; it's also a tool for achieving your long-term aspirations. This section delves into smart saving habits tailored for various goals, such as homeownership, education, or retirement. Explore strategies for setting up dedicated savings accounts, automating contributions, and leveraging investment vehicles to make your money work for you over time.

Investing for Future Growth: Beyond traditional savings accounts, we'll explore the world of investing as a powerful tool for long-term wealth accumulation. Understand the basics of investment vehicles such as stocks, bonds, and mutual funds, and discover how to create a diversified investment portfolio that aligns with your risk tolerance and financial goals.

Balancing Short-Term and Long-Term Savings: Finding the right balance between short-term and long-term savings is crucial for financial success. This section provides guidance on allocating your savings to address both immediate needs and future objectives. By adopting a strategic approach, you can ensure that your savings plan is comprehensive and adaptable to your evolving financial circumstances.

Automating Your Savings: Consistency is key when it comes to saving. Discover the benefits of automating your savings, whether through employer-sponsored retirement plans, automatic transfers to savings accounts, or investment contributions. Automation not only simplifies the saving process but also reinforces disciplined financial habits.

As we navigate through saving strategies, the goal is not only to accumulate wealth but also to foster a mindset of financial abundance. This chapter equips you with practical tools and insights to establish a robust savings plan, providing a solid foundation for achieving both short-term financial security and long-term financial success.

High-Yield Savings Accounts and Certificates of Deposit (CDs): Explore options beyond traditional savings accounts by delving into high-yield savings accounts and CDs. Understand the benefits, risks, and considerations associated with these alternatives. This section provides insights into maximizing interest earnings while maintaining liquidity, helping you make informed choices based on your financial goals.

Tax-Advantaged Savings: Certain savings vehicles offer tax advantages, providing an opportunity to optimize your overall financial strategy. Dive into the world of tax-advantaged savings accounts, such as 401(k)s, IRAs, and Health Savings Accounts (HSAs). Learn how these accounts can not only help you save for retirement and healthcare expenses but also provide tax benefits that contribute to long-term financial growth.

Savings Challenges and Games: Making saving enjoyable and engaging can be a powerful motivator. Discover the concept of savings challenges and games that turn the act of saving into a rewarding experience. From incremental challenges to financial games that involve goal-setting, these strategies add an element of fun to your savings journey while fostering discipline.

Mindful Spending and Saving: This section explores the connection between mindful spending and effective saving. By adopting mindful spending habits, you can identify areas where you can cut costs and redirect those funds towards your savings goals. Learn practical techniques for distinguishing between needs and wants, enabling you to make conscious financial decisions that align with your savings objectives.

Reviewing and Adjusting Savings Goals: Financial goals evolve over time, and so should your savings strategy. We'll discuss the importance of regularly reviewing and adjusting your savings goals based on changing circumstances, priorities, and life stages. This adaptive approach ensures that your savings plan remains aligned with your aspirations.

As you navigate through the diverse landscape of saving strategies, remember that saving is not just a financial activity; it's a mindset that empowers you to take control of your financial future. This chapter provides a comprehensive toolkit, allowing you to explore a variety of strategies and choose those that resonate best with your unique financial objectives and lifestyle.

CHAPTER 7
INVESTING FOR WEALTH

Investing is a powerful strategy for growing wealth over time and realizing long-term financial objectives. In this chapter, we will explore the principles, strategies, and considerations for effective wealth-building through investment.

Understanding Investment Vehicles: Begin by gaining a comprehensive understanding of various investment vehicles, including stocks, bonds, mutual funds, exchange-traded funds (ETFs), and real estate. This section will demystify the characteristics, risks, and potential returns associated with each, empowering you to make informed investment decisions aligned with your financial goals.

Building a Diversified Investment Portfolio:

Diversification is a cornerstone of prudent investing. Learn how to construct a well-balanced investment portfolio that spreads risk across different asset classes. We'll explore the concept of asset allocation, providing insights into how a diversified approach can enhance potential returns while mitigating the impact of market volatility.

Risk Tolerance and Investment Strategy:

Understanding your risk tolerance is crucial in designing an investment strategy that aligns with your financial goals and comfort level. This section explores the relationship between risk and reward, helping you define your risk tolerance and choose investment options that reflect your unique preferences and circumstances.

Long-Term vs. Short-Term Investing: Investing for wealth involves making strategic decisions about your investment horizon. Delve into the distinctions between long-term and short-term investing, exploring the benefits of each approach and understanding how your time horizon influences your investment choices.

Strategies for Market Downturns and Volatility: Markets are inherently unpredictable, and downturns are inevitable. Gain insights into strategies for navigating market volatility, including dollar-cost averaging, rebalancing, and maintaining a disciplined investment approach during turbulent times. Understanding how to weather market fluctuations is key to long-term wealth-building success.

Investment Monitoring and Adjustment: Effective wealth-building requires ongoing attention to your investment portfolio. Explore strategies for monitoring your investments, assessing performance, and making adjustments as needed. This proactive approach ensures that your portfolio remains aligned with your financial objectives and adapts to changes in the market and your personal circumstances.

As we explore the realm of investing for wealth, the goal is not only to grow your financial assets but also to do so in a manner that aligns with your individual goals, risk tolerance, and time horizon. This chapter equips you with the knowledge and tools to embark on a wealth-building journey through strategic and informed investment practices.

Research and Due Diligence: Before diving into investments, it's crucial to conduct thorough research and due diligence. Explore the importance of understanding the companies, industries, or funds you're investing in. This section provides practical tips for evaluating investment opportunities, analyzing financial statements, and staying informed about market trends.

Tax-Efficient Investing: Maximizing returns involves not just earning but also preserving your gains. Delve into the realm of tax-efficient investing, exploring strategies to minimize the impact of taxes on your investment returns. From tax-advantaged accounts to tax-efficient fund selection, this section provides insights into optimizing your investment strategy from a tax perspective.

The Role of Professional Advice: For many investors, seeking professional advice can be a prudent choice. Explore the role of financial advisors, wealth managers, and other professionals in guiding your investment decisions. Understand how to choose the right advisor, the services they provide, and how their expertise can complement your investment strategy.

Impact Investing and Sustainable Finance: An evolving trend in investing is the focus on environmental, social, and governance (ESG) factors. Discover the concept of impact investing and sustainable finance, where investors consider not only financial returns but also the social and environmental impact of their investments. Learn how aligning your investments with your values can contribute to both financial success and positive societal change.

Real Estate as an Investment Avenue: Real estate can be a tangible and lucrative investment option. Explore the world of real estate investment, including rental properties, real estate investment trusts (REITs), and property development. Understand the potential benefits and challenges of including real estate in your investment portfolio.

Retirement Investing Strategies: Investing for retirement is a unique facet of wealth-building. This section provides insights into retirement investing strategies, including employer-sponsored retirement plans, Individual Retirement Accounts (IRAs), and the concept of asset allocation tailored to retirement goals.

Learn how to structure your investments to support a comfortable and secure retirement.

By delving into these additional aspects of investing for wealth, you not only expand your knowledge but also enhance your ability to make strategic and informed investment decisions. Remember, the journey of wealth-building is dynamic, and adapting your investment approach to evolving circumstances is key to achieving enduring financial success.

CHAPTER 8
RETIREMENT PLANNING

Retirement planning is a critical element of financial mastery, ensuring that you can enjoy your post-work years comfortably and securely. In this chapter, we'll explore the principles, strategies, and considerations for effective retirement planning.

Securing Your Future: Retirement Savings

Strategies: Commence your journey into retirement planning by understanding the importance of saving for your future. Explore various retirement savings vehicles, including employer-sponsored plans like 401(k)s, Individual Retirement Accounts (IRAs), and other tax-advantaged options. Learn how to set realistic retirement savings goals and create a systematic plan to achieve them.

Navigating Retirement Investment Options:

Retirement investments require careful consideration. This section delves into the various investment options available within retirement accounts, from stocks and bonds to target-date funds. Understand how to tailor your investment portfolio to align with your retirement timeline, risk tolerance, and financial goals, ensuring that your assets grow efficiently over the long term.

Estimating Retirement Expenses: To plan effectively for retirement, you must have a clear understanding of your future expenses. Explore methods for estimating your retirement living costs, factoring in healthcare, housing, travel, and other potential expenditures. This section provides insights into creating a comprehensive budget that aligns with your lifestyle and retirement aspirations.

Decoding Social Security and Pension Plans: Social Security and pension plans are integral components of retirement income for many individuals. Understand how Social Security benefits are calculated, when to claim them, and strategies for optimizing your Social Security income. Additionally, explore the role of pension plans, if applicable, and how they contribute to your overall retirement income strategy.

Creating a Withdrawal Strategy: As you transition into retirement, the strategy for withdrawing funds from your retirement accounts becomes crucial. This section explores withdrawal strategies, including the 4% rule, systematic withdrawal plans, and considerations for tax efficiency. Learn how to strike a balance between enjoying your retirement and ensuring your financial sustainability throughout.

Longevity Planning and Healthcare: Longevity planning involves preparing for a potentially long and healthy retirement. Explore strategies for managing healthcare costs, including Medicare and supplemental insurance. Understand the role of long-term care planning and how it factors into your overall retirement strategy.

Retirement planning is a dynamic process that requires careful consideration and ongoing adjustments. This chapter provides you with the tools and insights needed to navigate the complexities of preparing for a financially secure and fulfilling retirement.

Income Sources in Retirement: Retirement income doesn't solely come from savings and investments. Explore the various income sources available during retirement, such as annuities, rental income, and part-time work. Understanding the diversity of income streams can enhance your financial security and flexibility during retirement.

Catch-Up Contributions and Late-stage Planning: For those who may have started saving for retirement later in their careers, catch-up contributions can be a valuable tool. Learn about the additional contributions allowed in certain retirement accounts and how they can boost your retirement savings during the final years of your working life.

Estate Planning and Legacy Considerations:

Retirement planning extends beyond your lifetime. Explore the importance of estate planning, including wills, trusts, and beneficiary designations. This section also delves into legacy considerations, helping you define how you want to pass on your wealth and values to future generations.

Inflation and Cost-of-Living Adjustments: Inflation can erode the purchasing power of your retirement income over time. Understand the impact of inflation on your retirement expenses and explore strategies for mitigating its effects. Learn about retirement accounts and investments that offer cost-of-living adjustments, helping your income keep pace with inflation.

Retirement Lifestyle Planning: Retirement isn't just about finances; it's also about lifestyle. This section encourages you to envision your ideal retirement lifestyle, whether it involves travel, hobbies, volunteering, or other pursuits. By aligning your financial plan with your lifestyle goals, you can create a retirement that is both financially secure and personally fulfilling.

Regular Retirement Checkups and Adjustments: Regular checkups are essential for maintaining your financial health in retirement. Explore the concept of regular retirement checkups, where you review your financial plan, assess your portfolio, and make adjustments as needed. This proactive approach ensures that your retirement plan remains aligned with your goals and adapts to changes in the economic landscape.

As you progress through the complexities of retirement planning, remember that it's a holistic process that involves financial, lifestyle, and legacy considerations. This chapter equips you with the knowledge and strategies to approach retirement planning comprehensively, ensuring that your post-work years are not only financially secure but also personally rewarding.

CHAPTER 9
INSURANCE ESSENTIALS FOR FINANCIAL SECURITY

Insurance plays a crucial role in safeguarding your financial well-being, providing protection against unexpected events that could otherwise derail your financial plans. In this chapter, we'll explore the essentials of insurance and how it contributes to your overall financial security.

Understanding the Basics: Types of Insurance: Start by gaining a comprehensive understanding of the various types of insurance. Explore essentials such as health insurance, life insurance, property and casualty insurance (including homeowners and auto insurance), and disability insurance. This section will provide insights into how each type of insurance contributes to different facets of your financial protection.

Health Insurance for Wellness and Financial Security: Health insurance is a cornerstone of your financial security. Delve into the intricacies of health insurance, including the importance of comprehensive coverage, understanding policy terms, and navigating healthcare networks. Learn how having the right health insurance can protect both your physical well-being and your financial assets.

Life Insurance as a Financial Safety Net: Life insurance is a crucial tool for providing financial protection to your loved ones in the event of your passing. Understand the different types of life insurance, such as term life and whole life, and how to determine the appropriate coverage for your unique circumstances. Explore how life insurance can also be utilized as an estate planning tool.

Property and Casualty Insurance: Safeguarding Your Assets: Your home, car, and other valuable assets require protection against unforeseen events. Explore the essentials of property and casualty insurance, including homeowners insurance, renters insurance, and auto insurance. Learn about coverage options, deductible considerations, and the role of insurance in mitigating financial losses due to accidents or natural disasters.

Disability Insurance: Protecting Your Income: Your ability to earn an income is a critical asset. Disability insurance provides a safety net in the event that you are unable to work due to illness or injury. Understand the key features of disability insurance, including benefit periods, elimination periods, and how to tailor coverage to your income and lifestyle.

Liability Insurance: Defending Against Legal Risks: Liability insurance protects you from financial consequences arising from legal claims. Explore how liability insurance, including umbrella insurance, can shield your assets in the event of lawsuits or liability claims. Understand coverage limits, the importance of liability coverage in various aspects of life, and how it contributes to overall financial security.

Regular Insurance Reviews: Adapting to Changing Circumstances: Insurance needs evolve over time. This section emphasizes the importance of regular insurance reviews, where you assess your coverage in light of changes in your life, such as marriage, the birth of children, home purchases, or career advancements. Regular reviews ensure that your insurance coverage remains adequate and aligned with your current circumstances.

As we explore insurance essentials, the goal is to view insurance not just as a mandatory expense but as a strategic tool for protecting your financial foundation. This chapter equips you with the knowledge to make informed decisions about the types and amounts of insurance coverage needed to create a comprehensive safety net for your financial security.

Long-Term Care Insurance: Planning for Future Healthcare Needs: As part of comprehensive insurance planning, consider the role of long-term care insurance.

Explore how this specialized insurance can help cover the costs associated with extended healthcare needs, including nursing home care, assisted living, and in-home care. Learn about the factors to consider when deciding if long-term care insurance is a valuable addition to your overall coverage.

Key Considerations in Selecting Insurance Policies: Choosing the right insurance policies involves careful consideration of various factors. This section provides a guide to key considerations when selecting insurance, including coverage limits, deductibles, policy exclusions, and the financial strength of insurance providers. Understanding these factors empowers you to make well-informed decisions that align with your financial goals.

Emergency Fund vs. Insurance Coverage: Finding the Balance: While insurance provides essential financial protection, maintaining an emergency fund is also crucial. Explore the balance between having adequate insurance coverage and the role of an emergency fund in handling smaller, more frequent financial setbacks. Learn how these two components work together to create a robust financial safety net.

Utilizing Risk Mitigation Strategies: Beyond Insurance: Risk mitigation involves strategies beyond traditional insurance. This section explores risk management techniques, such as risk avoidance, risk reduction, and risk retention. Understanding these strategies provides a holistic approach to managing risks in various areas of your life and financial portfolio.

Cybersecurity and Identity Theft Protection: Modern Insurance Considerations: In the digital age, safeguarding against cyber threats and identity theft is paramount. Explore the concept of cybersecurity insurance and identity theft protection. Learn about the coverage offered, preventive measures, and how these forms of insurance contribute to protecting your financial assets in an increasingly interconnected world.

Educating Yourself on Insurance Terms and Concepts: Insurance can be complex, with various terms and concepts unique to each type of coverage. This section serves as a glossary, providing explanations for common insurance terms. Empowering yourself with this knowledge enhances your ability to navigate the insurance landscape, ask informed questions, and make sound decisions.

Community and Government Insurance Programs: Supplementing Coverage: In addition to private insurance, explore community and government insurance programs that may supplement your coverage. This includes programs like Social Security, Medicare, and Medicaid. Understanding the role of these programs in your overall insurance strategy contributes to a comprehensive approach to financial security.

By delving into these additional aspects of insurance essentials, you not only broaden your understanding of various coverage options but also enhance your ability to create a customized insurance strategy that aligns with your unique financial circumstances and goals.

CHAPTER 10

TAX PLANNING FOR FINANCIAL OPTIMIZATION

Tax planning is a fundamental component of financial mastery, allowing you to minimize your tax liability and optimize your overall financial strategy. In this chapter, we'll explore the essentials of tax planning and how it intersects with your broader financial goals.

Understanding the Tax Landscape: Types of Taxes and Their Implications: Start by gaining a comprehensive understanding of the various types of taxes, including income taxes, capital gains taxes, estate taxes, and more. Explore how each type of tax impacts your financial situation and the importance of aligning your tax strategy with your overall financial plan.

Strategic Income Management: Timing and Deferring Income: Explore strategies for managing your income strategically to minimize tax implications. This section delves into concepts such as income deferral, timing of income recognition, and leveraging tax-advantaged accounts. Learn how these strategies can contribute to lowering your overall tax burden.

Maximizing Deductions and Credits: Leveraging Tax Benefits: Deductions and credits are valuable tools in tax planning. Discover common deductions and credits available to individuals, such as those related to homeownership, education expenses, and energy-efficient improvements. Understand how to maximize these benefits to reduce your taxable income and potentially receive tax refunds.

Investment Strategies for Tax Efficiency: Capitalizing on Tax Advantages: Investing with tax efficiency in mind is crucial for optimizing returns. Explore investment strategies, including tax-loss harvesting, holding investments for the long term to benefit from lower capital gains rates, and utilizing tax-advantaged accounts like IRAs and 401(k)s. Learn how these strategies can enhance your after-tax investment returns.

Estate Planning and Inheritance Taxes: Preserving Wealth Across Generations: Estate planning is not only about passing on wealth but also minimizing the impact of estate and inheritance taxes. Understand the basics of estate planning, including the use of trusts, gifting strategies, and other tools to preserve assets for future generations while minimizing tax liabilities.

Tax-Advantaged Accounts and Retirement Planning: Securing Your Future Tax-Efficiently: Explore the role of tax-advantaged accounts in retirement planning, such as Traditional and Roth IRAs, 401(k)s, and Health Savings Accounts (HSAs). Understand how contributions, withdrawals, and investment growth within these accounts can have different tax implications, allowing you to strategically plan for your financial future.

Tax Planning for Small Business Owners: Strategies for Entrepreneurs: For small business owners, tax planning is integral to financial success. Explore tax-saving strategies specific to entrepreneurs, including business deductions, credits, and retirement planning options. Understand how structuring your business appropriately can contribute to both operational efficiency and tax optimization.

Regular Tax Reviews and Adjustments: Adapting to Changes in Tax Laws: The tax landscape is dynamic, with laws and regulations subject to change. Regular tax reviews are essential for adapting your tax strategy to new circumstances. Explore the importance of staying informed about tax law changes, working with tax professionals, and making adjustments to your financial plan as needed.

By delving into these aspects of tax planning, you not only optimize your current tax situation but also position yourself strategically for future financial success. This chapter provides insights and strategies to empower you to make informed decisions that align with your broader

financial goals while minimizing your tax burden.

Charitable Giving and Tax Benefits: Combining Philanthropy with Tax Efficiency: Explore the intersection of charitable giving and tax planning. Learn about tax benefits associated with donations to qualified charities, including deductions and strategies for maximizing the impact of your philanthropic efforts while minimizing your tax liability.

Education Planning and Tax-Advantaged Accounts: Investing in the Future Tax-Efficiently: For those with educational goals, tax planning extends to education savings. Delve into tax-advantaged accounts such as 529 plans and Coverdell Education Savings Accounts (ESAs). Understand how these accounts offer tax benefits while helping you save for educational expenses.

Healthcare Planning and Tax-Advantaged Health Savings Accounts (HSAs): Healthcare expenses are a significant part of many individuals' budgets. Explore the tax advantages of Health Savings Accounts (HSAs), including contributions, withdrawals, and investment growth. Learn how HSAs provide a triple tax benefit, making them a powerful tool for managing both current and future healthcare costs.

Tax Implications of Real Estate Transactions: Buying, Selling, and Investing Wisely: Real estate transactions have notable tax implications. Explore the tax considerations when buying, selling, or investing in real estate. Understand deductions related to mortgage interest and property taxes, as well as the capital gains implications of selling property. Learn how strategic decisions in real estate can align with your overall tax plan.

Tax-Efficient Withdrawal Strategies in Retirement: Creating a Tax-Smart Retirement Income Plan: As you transition into retirement, how you withdraw funds from your various accounts can impact your tax liability. Explore tax-efficient withdrawal strategies, including the order in which you tap into different types of retirement accounts. Understand how careful planning can optimize your after-tax income in retirement.

Tax Planning for Stock Options and Equity Compensation: Managing Complex Assets: For individuals with stock options and equity compensation, tax planning is particularly complex. Explore strategies for managing the tax implications of stock options, restricted stock units (RSUs), and other forms of equity compensation. Understand the timing and methods of exercising options to optimize tax outcomes.

Tax Consequences of Business Transactions: Mergers, Acquisitions, and Sales: For business owners involved in transactions such as mergers, acquisitions, or sales, understanding the tax consequences is essential. Explore the tax implications of these business transactions, including considerations for structuring deals to optimize tax outcomes.

Tax Planning for International Income and Investments: Navigating Global Tax Complexity: In an increasingly globalized world, individuals with international income or investments face unique tax challenges. Explore the tax implications of international activities, including income earned abroad, foreign investments, and adherence to tax treaties. Understand how to navigate the complexity of international tax laws to optimize your overall tax strategy.

By delving into these nuanced aspects of tax planning, you not only enhance your understanding of various tax considerations but also develop a comprehensive tax strategy that aligns with your unique financial circumstances and long-term goals. This chapter provides a detailed roadmap for navigating the intricacies of tax planning for financial optimization.

CHAPTER 11
FINANCIAL MILESTONES: A ROAD MAP TO SUCCESS

Financial milestones serve as markers on your journey to financial mastery, providing guidance, motivation, and a tangible measure of your progress. In this chapter, we'll explore key financial milestones and how they relate to the broader context of financial planning and optimization.

Building Emergency Savings: The Foundation Milestone: The journey toward financial mastery often begins with the establishment of an emergency savings fund. This foundational milestone serves as a safety net, providing financial security in the face of unexpected expenses or disruptions. Learn about setting realistic savings goals and gradually building an emergency fund that aligns with your lifestyle and needs.

Debt-Free Living: Liberation from Financial Obligations: Achieving freedom from high-interest debt is a significant financial milestone. This chapter explores strategies for managing and eliminating debt, from credit cards to student loans. Learn how a debt-free status not only relieves financial stress but also opens up opportunities for saving, investing, and pursuing your long-term goals.

Establishing a Solid Credit Score: The Gateway to Financial Opportunities: A strong credit score is a key to unlocking various financial opportunities. Explore the factors that contribute to a good credit score, the importance of credit reports, and strategies for building and maintaining healthy credit. Learn how a solid credit score can facilitate favorable terms on loans, mortgages, and other financial transactions.

Homeownership: A Milestone of Stability and Investment: Owning a home is a significant financial milestone for many. This section explores the considerations involved in purchasing a home, from saving for a down payment to navigating the mortgage process. Understand how homeownership can contribute to stability, wealth-building, and long-term financial security.

Investing for the Future: The Wealth Accumulation Milestone: Embarking on the journey of investing marks a pivotal financial milestone. Explore the principles of investing, from understanding risk tolerance to constructing a diversified portfolio. Learn how investing can contribute to wealth accumulation, retirement planning, and the achievement of long-term financial goals.

Retirement Savings: Securing Your Future Lifestyle: Building a robust retirement savings plan is a cornerstone of financial success. This chapter explores retirement milestones, including reaching specific savings targets and strategically planning for the transition into retirement. Learn how compound growth, tax advantages, and strategic investment choices contribute to a financially secure retirement.

Education Funding: Investing in Knowledge and Future Generations: Saving for education expenses is a key milestone for individuals with children or those pursuing further education themselves. Explore strategies for funding education, including tax-advantaged accounts like 529 plans. Learn how proactive planning can alleviate the financial burden of educational pursuits.

Achieving Financial Independence: The Ultimate Milestone: Financial independence represents the pinnacle of financial success. Explore the concept of financial independence, where your passive income covers your living expenses. Learn about the principles of the FIRE (Financial Independence, Retire Early) movement and how achieving financial independence provides the freedom to design the life you desire.

Legacy Planning: Leaving a Lasting Impact: As you progress through financial milestones, legacy planning becomes a consideration. This section explores strategies for preserving and passing on wealth to future generations. Learn about estate planning, charitable giving, and the creation of a lasting legacy that aligns with your values and financial aspirations.

By understanding and working toward these financial milestones, you not only create a roadmap for your financial journey but also cultivate habits and strategies that contribute to lasting financial success. This chapter serves as a guide to navigating the various stages of financial mastery, from foundational steps to the attainment of financial independence and beyond.

Healthcare and Insurance Milestones: Safeguarding Your Well-Being: As you progress in your financial journey, achieving milestones in healthcare and insurance is essential. This section explores milestones such as obtaining comprehensive health insurance, establishing a robust healthcare savings plan, and understanding the role of insurance in protecting your financial well-being. Learn how proactive healthcare planning contributes to overall financial security.

Career Advancement and Income Growth: Elevating Your Financial Potential: Advancing in your career and experiencing income growth are significant financial milestones. Explore strategies for career development, negotiating salary increases, and diversifying income streams. Learn how maximizing your earning potential contributes to achieving various financial goals and milestones.

Business Ownership and Entrepreneurial Milestones: Creating Financial Independence: For aspiring entrepreneurs, milestones related to business ownership are pivotal. This section explores milestones such as launching a business, achieving profitability, and expanding operations. Understand how entrepreneurship can contribute to financial independence and the ability to shape your professional and financial destiny.

Tax Efficiency Milestones: Optimizing Your Tax Strategy: Achieving milestones in tax efficiency is crucial for maximizing your financial resources. Explore milestones such as mastering strategic income management, utilizing tax-advantaged accounts, and implementing tax-efficient investment strategies. Learn how a proactive approach to tax planning enhances your overall financial optimization.

Philanthropy and Charitable Giving: Leaving a Positive Impact: As your financial journey evolves, milestones in philanthropy and charitable giving become meaningful. Explore strategies for incorporating charitable giving into your financial plan, leveraging tax benefits, and leaving a positive impact on causes you care about. Learn how philanthropy aligns with your values and contributes to a sense of purpose in your financial success.

Travel and Lifestyle Milestones: Enjoying the Fruits of Financial Success: Achieving financial milestones isn't solely about planning for the future; it's also about enjoying the present. This section explores milestones related to travel, lifestyle enhancements, and pursuing personal passions. Learn how balancing present enjoyment with future planning contributes to a fulfilling and well-rounded financial journey.

Financial Education and Literacy Milestones: Empowering Your Knowledge Base: Continual financial education is a vital milestone in achieving long-term financial success. Explore milestones related to expanding your financial literacy, staying informed about market trends, and understanding complex financial concepts. Learn how an ongoing commitment to learning enhances your ability to make informed financial decisions.

Mindful Spending and Budgeting Mastery: Achieving Financial Balance: Mastering the art of mindful spending and budgeting is a cornerstone of financial well-being. This section explores milestones such as creating a realistic budget, practicing mindful spending habits, and achieving a healthy balance between saving and enjoying life. Learn how these milestones contribute to sustained financial stability and peace of mind.

Adapting to Life Transitions: Flexibility in Financial Planning: Life is full of transitions, and adapting your financial plan to changing circumstances is a crucial milestone. Explore milestones related to life events such as marriage, parenthood, job changes, and unexpected challenges. Learn how flexibility and adaptability in financial planning contribute to resilience and long-term success.

By recognizing and working towards these diverse financial milestones, you create a comprehensive roadmap for your financial journey. Each milestone contributes to a holistic and adaptive approach to

financial mastery, fostering a sense of empowerment and

achievement at every stage of your financial life.

CHAPTER 12
MAINTAINING FINANCIAL HEALTH: SUSTAINING SUCCESS

Maintaining financial health is an ongoing commitment that involves the consistent application of sound financial principles. In this chapter, we'll explore strategies and practices for sustaining your financial success and navigating the complexities of long-term financial well-being.

Regular Financial Checkups: Monitoring Your Financial Vital Signs: Just as you prioritize regular health checkups, consistent financial checkups are essential. This section delves into the importance of periodic reviews of your financial plan, budget, and investment portfolio. Learn how regular assessments help you identify areas for improvement, adapt to changing circumstances, and stay on track toward your financial goals.

Emergency Fund Maintenance: Ensuring Financial Resilience: An adequately funded emergency savings account is the cornerstone of financial resilience. Explore strategies for maintaining and replenishing your emergency fund over time. Learn how changes in income, expenses, and life circumstances may impact your fund requirements, and adjust accordingly to ensure you're prepared for unexpected financial challenges.

Debt Management Strategies: Continual Improvement and Elimination: Managing debt is an ongoing process. This section explores strategies for continually improving your debt management approach, whether it's through refinancing, negotiating lower interest rates, or accelerating debt repayment. Learn how a proactive stance toward debt contributes to long-term financial health.

Investment Portfolio Rebalancing: Adapting to Market Changes: Investment portfolios require periodic rebalancing to align with your risk tolerance and financial goals. Explore the principles of portfolio rebalancing, understanding when and how to adjust your investments based on changes in market conditions and your personal circumstances. Learn how this proactive approach contributes to sustained investment success.

Expense Tracking and Budgeting Refinement: Fine-Tuning Your Financial Habits: Maintaining financial health involves continual refinement of your spending habits. This section explores advanced budgeting techniques, including detailed expense tracking, categorization, and analysis. Learn how fine-tuning your budget allows you to make informed decisions, identify potential savings, and allocate resources more effectively.

Lifestyle Adjustments and Financial Adaptability:

Responding to Changes: Life is dynamic, and financial health requires adaptability. Explore strategies for adjusting your lifestyle and financial plan in response to changes such as job transitions, family additions, or shifts in personal goals. Learn how flexibility in your approach to finance contributes to long-term sustainability.

Tax Planning Updates: Staying Informed and Compliant: Tax laws and regulations change, necessitating regular updates to your tax planning strategy. This section explores the importance of staying informed about tax changes, working with tax professionals, and making adjustments to optimize your tax strategy. Learn how a proactive approach to tax planning contributes to ongoing financial efficiency.

Continued Education and Skill Development:

Enhancing Financial Literacy: Financial literacy is a lifelong journey. This chapter emphasizes the importance of continued education and skill development in financial matters. Explore resources for expanding your financial knowledge, staying informed about economic trends, and adapting to advancements in financial technology. Learn how a commitment to ongoing learning enhances your financial decision-making capabilities.

Community Engagement and Networking:

Leveraging Collective Wisdom: Engaging with your community and networking with peers can be valuable for maintaining financial health. This section explores the benefits of sharing experiences, seeking advice, and learning from the collective wisdom of your community. Learn how building a network of financial support contributes to your overall financial well-being.

Mindful Spending Practices: Balancing Enjoyment and Financial Goals: Mindful spending practices go beyond budgeting; they involve cultivating a balanced approach to enjoying life while pursuing financial goals. Explore strategies for aligning your spending with your values, distinguishing between needs and wants, and making intentional financial decisions. Learn how mindful spending contributes to both financial satisfaction and long-term success.

By embracing these practices and strategies for maintaining financial health, you not only sustain the success you've achieved but also foster a mindset of continual improvement and adaptability. This chapter serves as a guide to navigating the ongoing journey of financial well-being.

Regular Retirement Checkups: Adapting to Changing Goals and Market Conditions: As you progress through life, your retirement goals and circumstances may evolve. Regular retirement checkups involve reviewing your retirement savings plan, investment portfolio, and withdrawal strategy. Explore strategies for adapting to changes in retirement goals, market conditions, and personal circumstances. Learn how ongoing assessment ensures that your retirement plan remains aligned with your aspirations.

Insurance Coverage Reviews: Aligning Protection with Life Changes: Insurance needs evolve over time, making regular coverage reviews essential. This section explores the importance of assessing your health, life, property, and other insurance coverage in light of life changes. Learn how to update policies, add coverage as needed, and ensure that your insurance protection remains in sync with your current circumstances.

Legacy Planning Updates: Adapting to Changing Family Dynamics: Legacy planning is a dynamic process that requires periodic updates. Explore strategies for adapting your estate plan, wills, trusts, and beneficiary designations to changing family dynamics, financial circumstances, and legal considerations. Learn how to ensure that your legacy plan reflects your current wishes and provides for future generations.

Technology and Security Audits: Safeguarding Your Financial Information: In the digital age, maintaining financial health involves safeguarding your information from cyber threats. Explore the importance of technology and security audits, including securing online accounts, using secure networks, and staying informed about cybersecurity best practices. Learn how proactive measures contribute to the protection of your financial assets.

Continual Debt Reduction: Striving for Financial Freedom: While achieving debt freedom is a milestone, continual debt reduction is an ongoing process. Explore advanced strategies for accelerating debt payoff, negotiating lower interest rates, and optimizing your debt management approach. Learn how a proactive stance toward debt contributes to sustained financial freedom.

Real Estate Portfolio Management: Leveraging Property Investments: For those with real estate investments, managing your portfolio is an ongoing responsibility. Explore strategies for optimizing rental properties, evaluating market conditions, and making informed decisions about property acquisitions or sales. Learn how effective real estate portfolio management contributes to overall financial health and wealth-building.

Family Financial Discussions: Fostering Open Communication: Maintaining financial health involves open communication within your family. Explore the benefits of regular family financial discussions, including setting financial goals, addressing concerns, and making joint decisions. Learn how fostering a culture of financial transparency contributes to a unified approach to financial well-being.

Regular Credit Score Monitoring: Protecting Your Financial Reputation: Your credit score is a critical component of your financial health. Explore strategies for regular credit score monitoring, understanding the factors that impact your score, and addressing any discrepancies or issues promptly. Learn how a proactive approach to credit management contributes to favorable financial outcomes.

Mindfulness Practices for Financial Well-Being: Balancing Stress and Financial Health: The connection between mental well-being and financial health is significant. This section explores mindfulness practices, stress reduction techniques, and strategies for maintaining a healthy mindset about finances. Learn how cultivating a positive relationship with money contributes to overall financial well-being.

Financial Wellness Programs and Resources: Accessing Supportive Tools: Many organizations offer financial wellness programs and resources to support individuals in maintaining financial health. Explore the benefits of these programs, including budgeting tools, financial education resources, and counseling services. Learn how leveraging available resources contributes to sustained financial well-being.

By integrating these practices into your ongoing financial management, you not only maintain the success you've achieved but also foster a resilient and adaptable approach to financial well-being. This chapter serves as a guide to navigating the complexities of continual financial health and growth

CHAPTER 13
BUILDING GENERATIONAL WEALTH: A LEGACY OF FINANCIAL SUCCESS

Building generational wealth involves strategic financial planning that extends beyond individual achievements to create a lasting impact on future generations. In this chapter, we'll explore the principles and strategies for building generational wealth and leaving a legacy of financial success.

Foundations of Generational Wealth: Setting the Stage for Success: Generational wealth begins with a solid foundation. This section explores the importance of financial literacy, education, and instilling strong values around money within the family. Learn how these foundational elements set the stage for building and preserving wealth across generations.

Strategic Family Financial Planning: Collaborative Goal Setting: Building generational wealth requires a collaborative approach to family financial planning. Explore strategies for involving family members in goal setting, creating a shared vision for the future, and fostering open communication about financial matters. Learn how a united family front contributes to the long-term success of generational wealth planning.

Education and Skill Development: Empowering Future Generations: Empowering future generations involves providing them with the knowledge and skills to navigate the financial landscape. This section explores strategies for supporting education and skill development, including funding educational pursuits, mentorship, and real-world financial experiences. Learn how investing in the capabilities of the next generation contributes to the growth of generational wealth.

Real Estate and Property Investments: Building Tangible Assets: Real estate has long been a cornerstone of generational wealth. Explore strategies for acquiring and managing real estate investments, including rental properties, commercial ventures, and land holdings. Learn how a carefully curated real estate portfolio can serve as a tangible asset for future generations.

Creating and Managing Trusts: Preserving Wealth Across Time: Trusts are powerful tools for preserving and managing wealth across generations. This section explores the principles of creating and managing trusts, including revocable and irrevocable trusts. Learn how trusts provide a structured and tax-efficient way to pass on assets while maintaining control and flexibility.

Entrepreneurship and Business Succession Planning: Passing Down Ventures: For families involved in entrepreneurship, planning for the succession of businesses is crucial. Explore strategies for business succession planning, including grooming successors, establishing clear governance structures, and navigating tax implications. Learn how the successful transition of family businesses contributes to the continuity of generational wealth.

Investment Strategies for Long-Term Growth: Compound Growth and Diversification: Long-term investment strategies are key to generational wealth. This section explores the principles of compound growth, diversification, and strategic investment planning. Learn how a well-managed investment portfolio can generate sustainable returns over the years, contributing to the growth of family wealth.

Tax Planning Across Generations: Minimizing Tax Implications: Effective tax planning is essential for preserving generational wealth. Explore strategies for minimizing tax implications across generations, including considerations for estate taxes, gift taxes, and capital gains taxes. Learn how a proactive approach to tax planning enhances the longevity and impact of generational wealth.

Philanthropy and Social Responsibility: Embedding Values in Wealth: Generational wealth goes beyond financial assets; it includes the values and principles that shape a family's legacy. This section explores the role of philanthropy and social responsibility in generational wealth planning. Learn how embedding values in wealth contributes to a legacy that extends beyond monetary assets.

Regular Family Financial Checkups: Adapting to Changing Circumstances: As circumstances evolve, regular family financial checkups become essential for adjusting generational wealth plans. Explore the importance of adapting to changing economic conditions, family dynamics, and individual goals. Learn how ongoing assessments contribute to the resilience and sustainability of generational wealth.

Building generational wealth is a dynamic and intentional process that requires careful planning, education, and a commitment to shared values. This chapter provides insights and strategies to empower families in creating a lasting legacy of financial success that spans across generations.

Strategies for Financial Education Across Generations: Knowledge Transfer: The transfer of financial knowledge across generations is a critical aspect of building generational wealth. Explore strategies for facilitating knowledge transfer within the family, including financial education programs, mentorship, and shared experiences. Learn how empowering each generation with financial literacy enhances their ability to contribute to the growth of family wealth.

Cultivating Entrepreneurial Spirit: Nurturing Innovation and Leadership: For families with an entrepreneurial spirit, cultivating this mindset across generations is essential. This section explores strategies for nurturing innovation, leadership, and entrepreneurial ventures within the family. Learn how encouraging creativity and a proactive approach to business can contribute to sustained financial success.

Multigenerational Investment Committees: Collaborative Wealth Management: Managing generational wealth often involves the creation of multigenerational investment committees. Explore the benefits of collaborative wealth management, where family members collectively make investment decisions, set financial goals, and ensure alignment with the family's long-term vision. Learn how this approach fosters unity and shared responsibility in financial stewardship.

Social Capital and Networking: Expanding Opportunities Through Connections: Building generational wealth extends beyond financial assets to include social capital. This section explores the importance of networking and establishing connections within and outside the family. Learn how leveraging social capital can open doors to new opportunities, partnerships, and ventures that contribute to the expansion of family wealth.

Environmental, Social, and Governance (ESG) Investing: Aligning Values with Investments: Incorporating environmental, social, and governance (ESG) considerations into investment strategies aligns family wealth with broader societal values. Explore how ESG investing can be a powerful tool for building generational wealth with a focus on sustainability, ethical practices, and positive social impact.

Intergenerational Real Estate Planning: Legacy Properties and Family Retreats: Real estate planning across generations involves the strategic management of family properties and the creation of legacy estates. This section explores the benefits of maintaining family retreats, vacation homes, and legacy properties. Learn how inter-generational real estate planning contributes to the preservation of family traditions and wealth.

Creating Family Constitutions: Establishing Governance Structures: To ensure continuity and effective decision-making, families often create family constitutions or governance structures. Explore the principles of establishing family constitutions, including defining roles, responsibilities, and dispute resolution processes. Learn how these structures provide a framework for maintaining unity and preserving generational wealth.

Incorporating Philanthropy into Family Values: Charitable Giving Strategies: Generational wealth often includes a commitment to philanthropy. This section explores strategies for incorporating charitable giving into family values, establishing family foundations, and engaging in impactful philanthropic initiatives. Learn how philanthropy becomes a central component of the family legacy.

Teaching Financial Resilience: Preparing for Economic Challenges: Equipping future generations with financial resilience is crucial for navigating economic challenges. Explore strategies for teaching financial resilience, including instilling a strong work ethic, fostering adaptability, and providing tools for overcoming setbacks. Learn how these lessons contribute to the family's ability to weather economic uncertainties and preserve generational wealth.

Continual Legal and Estate Planning Updates: Adapting to Changing Laws: Legal and estate planning require ongoing attention to adapt to changing laws and family circumstances. This section explores the importance of regular updates to legal documents, wills, and trusts. Learn how staying abreast of legal changes ensures that the family's wealth transfer strategies remain effective and compliant.

Building generational wealth is a dynamic and multifaceted endeavor that requires a thoughtful and integrated approach. This chapter provides additional insights and strategies to empower families in creating a lasting legacy of financial success that spans across generations.

CONCLUSION:

Sustaining the Flame of Generational

Prosperity; Building generational wealth is not merely a financial pursuit; it's a commitment to creating a legacy that transcends time. As we conclude this exploration into strategies for building and sustaining generational wealth, it's evident that the journey involves a delicate blend of financial acumen, shared values, and a forward-thinking mindset.

The foundation of generational wealth lies in education—equipping each family member with the knowledge and skills to navigate the complex terrain of finance. Through financial education programs, mentor-ship, and hands-on experiences, families can empower successive generations to make informed decisions and contribute to the growth of family wealth.

Collaboration is another key pillar. Establishing family governance structures, conducting regular family meetings, and involving members in financial decision-making foster a sense of unity. Multi-generational investment committees, where family members collectively steer the course of investments, exemplify the strength that comes from shared responsibility.

In the realm of investments, a diversified and long-term approach is fundamental. Whether through real estate holdings, entrepreneurial ventures, or strategic philanthropy, families can tailor their investment portfolios to align with both financial goals and shared values. Environmental, social, and governance (ESG) considerations have emerged as integral factors, reflecting a commitment to sustainability and ethical practices.

The importance of adaptability cannot be overstated. Legal and estate planning require continual updates to accommodate changes in laws and family dynamics. The ability to navigate economic challenges with resilience, fostered through financial education and a culture of innovation, ensures the family's capacity to weather uncertainties and preserve generational wealth.

Philanthropy, too, plays a central role. Beyond financial assets, families can contribute to societal well-being by integrating philanthropic initiatives into their values. By aligning charitable giving with shared causes, families not only make a positive impact on the world but also instill a sense of purpose that transcends financial success.

As families embark on the journey of building generational wealth, they embark on a legacy-building mission—one that goes beyond numbers on a balance sheet. It's a journey of empowerment, resilience, and interconnectedness. Through intentional planning, continuous education, and a commitment to shared values, families have the opportunity to sustain the flame of prosperity across generations, leaving an enduring legacy for the benefit of posterity.

In embracing the principles outlined in this exploration, families lay the groundwork for a future where each generation builds upon the successes of the previous one, perpetuating a cycle of prosperity that extends far beyond individual lifetimes. The legacy of generational wealth is not only in what is amassed but in the values instilled, the knowledge shared, and the positive impact left on the world—a testament to a family's enduring commitment to prosperity, both financial and beyond.

Nurturing the Seeds of Generational Prosperity

In concluding our exploration of strategies for building generational wealth, it becomes clear that the journey is a dynamic tapestry woven with threads of financial wisdom, shared values, and a commitment to a legacy that echoes through time. The conclusion of this chapter extends an invitation to families embarking on this enduring quest to reflect on the deeper aspects of generational prosperity.

Cultivating Financial Wisdom: A Beacon for Future Generations: Generational wealth is not solely about accumulating financial assets but about cultivating a legacy of financial wisdom. As families impart knowledge through education, workshops, and shared experiences, they are sowing the seeds of financial acumen that will blossom in the generations to come. It's a beacon that guides family members in navigating the complexities of the financial landscape, making informed decisions, and contributing to the perpetuation of prosperity.

Unity Through Shared Responsibility: Crafting a Tapestry of Collaboration: A central theme emerges — the significance of unity through shared responsibility. Families that create structures for collaborative decision-making, such as multi-generational investment committees and family constitutions, weave a tapestry of unity. In doing so, they foster a sense of shared responsibility that not only safeguards the family's financial interests but also strengthens the bonds that tie successive generations together.

Innovation and Adaptability: Navigating the Ebb and Flow of Time: As families plan for the long term, they recognize the impermanence of circumstances. The conclusion of our discussion underscores the importance of innovation and adaptability. Families that embrace entrepreneurial spirit, engage in continual legal and estate planning updates, and teach the value of resilience are better equipped to navigate the ebb and flow of time. They stand resilient in the face of economic changes, ensuring that the flame of generational prosperity endures.

Philanthropy as a Legacy of Impact: Beyond Wealth, a Contribution to Humanity: Generational wealth extends beyond the confines of family assets. It manifests in philanthropy — a legacy of impact on the broader community and the world. Families that integrate philanthropy into their values contribute to causes that resonate with their collective mission. In doing so, they weave a narrative of not only financial success but also a positive imprint on the world, leaving a lasting legacy of compassion and social responsibility.

Sustainability Through Diversification: Nurturing a Resilient Financial Ecosystem: The conclusion of our exploration emphasizes the sustainability that comes through diversification. Families that strategically diversify their investments, embracing a blend of real estate, entrepreneurship, and thoughtful philanthropy, nurture a resilient financial ecosystem. This diversified approach ensures that the family's wealth not only endures but also adapts to the changing dynamics of the world.

A Tapestry Woven with Values: Crafting a Timeless Legacy: In conclusion, building generational wealth is akin to crafting a timeless tapestry woven with values, knowledge, and a commitment to prosperity. It is a journey that transcends generations, leaving an indelible mark on the family's narrative. The legacy is not merely financial; it is a testament to the enduring spirit of the family, a beacon that illuminates the path for generations to come.

As families embark on this profound journey, they are invited to reflect not only on the wealth they accumulate but on the values they instill, the knowledge they share, and the impact they make. The conclusion of our exploration serves as a reminder that the true essence of generational wealth lies in the intangibles — the stories told, the lessons learned, and the enduring spirit of prosperity that weaves through the fabric of time.